Look out

by

Water

RED RAINBOWS

The Caterpillar Story
Houses and Homes
Look out at Home
Look out by Water
Look out for Strangers
Look out on the Road
Looking Around
My Senses
Old and New
Sun's Hot, Sea's Cold
What People Do

What's the Weather?
When Dad was Young
When Grandma was Young
My Christian Faith*
Fy Fydd Gristnogol (Welsh edition)*
My Hindu Faith*
My Jewish Faith*
My Muslim Faith*
My Sikh Faith*
My Buddhist Faith*
*Also available as Big Books

EDUCATIONAL AND READING CONSULTANT

Cardy Moxley, Advisory Teacher for Reading and Language,
Hereford and Worcester

First published in paperback in 2003

SAFETY CONSULTANT

Checked by the Safety Advisor at the Royal Society for the Prevention of
Accidents (RoSPA), RoSPA House, Edgbaston Park, 353 Bristol Road,
Birmingham B5 7ST

Published by Evans Brothers Limited
2A Portman Mansions
Chiltern Street
London W1U 6NR

First published in 1994
Reprinted in 1997
Printed in Hong Kong by Wing King Tong Co., Ltd

ISBN 0237 52543 7

ACKNOWLEDGEMENTS
Planned and produced by The Creative Publishing Company
Picture Research by Helena Ramsay
Designed by Rafi Mohamed
Typesetting by Colour Bytes Ltd.

For permission to reproduce copyright material the author and publishers
gratefully acknowledge the following:
Greg Evans International: pages 7, 23; Chris Fairclough: pages 19, 25;
Alex Ramsay: page 21; Tony Stone: pages 9,15

Look out by Water

Helena Ramsay

Illustrated by
Colin King

Evans

You must always have a grown-up with you when you are near water.
Never go on your own.

The ground is often slippery near water. If you run, you might fall over and hurt yourself.

7

Never behave in a silly way
when you are near water.
There might be
an accident.

Never jump or dive into water unless you know how deep it is.

Always find a safe place to get in and out of the water.

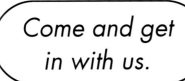

Come and get in with us.

It's safe here. We can see the bottom.

13

The water can get deeper
very suddenly at the seaside.
Be careful never to get out
of your depth.

I can swim in the deep end at the swimming pool.

The sea can have very
strong currents.
If you got out of your
depth, the current might
pull you away.

It's dangerous to play on air beds at the seaside. You might be pulled out to sea by the current.

19

Never swim in rivers and lakes, it's too dangerous.

The current carried my toy boat away.

The tide can come in very quickly.

Always take care not to be cut off from the beach by deep water.

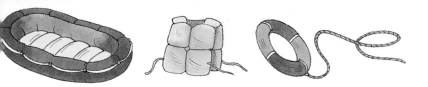

Everybody should wear a
life-jacket when they go
on a boat.

Water can be dangerous,
even if you know how
to swim.

Everybody sit down, please!

If you don't do as you are told on a boat you might fall into the water.

And so have I. You've all been very good.

Always be sensible when you are near water and you'll have lots of fun.

Some of these children are being sensible near water and some are being silly. Do you know which are which?

Index

The Water Safety Code

To keep yourself safe, when you are in, on or beside water, always follow the Water Safety Code.

Spot the dangers!

Water may look safe, but it can be dangerous. Learn to spot and stay away from dangers. You may swim well in a warm indoor pool, but that does not mean that you will be able to swim in cold water.

The dangers of water include: it is very cold; it can be very deep; it is difficult to estimate depth; there may be hidden currents; there may be hidden rubbish, e.g. shopping trolleys, broken glass; it may be polluted and may make you ill; it can be difficult to get out (steep slimy banks); there are no lifeguards.

Take safety advice!

Special flags and notices may warn you of danger. Know what the signs mean and what they tell you.

Don't go alone!

Children should always go with an adult, not by themselves. An adult can point out dangers or help if somebody gets into trouble.

Learn how to help!

You may be able to help yourself and others if you know what to do in an emergency. If you see someone in difficulty, tell somebody, preferably a Lifeguard if there is one nearby, or go to the nearest telephone, dial **999**, ask for the **Police** at inland water sites and the **Coastguard** at the beach.